Macramè

The Ultimate Step by Step Illustrated
Guide to Learn the Secrets of
Macramé + 15 Project Ideas for
Beginners to Boost your Creativity.

Jessie Crafts

Books of the Same Author

1. Cricut Complete Guide (4 Books in 1)

2. Cricut Air Explore 2

3. Cricut Project Ideas

4. Cricut Maker For Beginners

5. Cricut Design Space

6. Complete Guide To Cricut 2 Volumes

including, without limitation, warranties of merchantability, fitness for a particular purpose and non-infringement.

This book may contain advices, opinions and statements from various information providers. It does not represent or endorse the accuracy or reliability of the suggestions, opinions, declarations or other information provided by any information provider, any reader or any other person or entity. Trust in any advice, opinion, statement or other information will also be at the risk and expense of the reader. Neither the owner nor the author will be responsible to the reader or any other person for any inaccuracy, error, omission, interruption, elimination, defect, alteration or use of any content in this document, or for its timeliness or integrity.

Table of Contents

Introduction to Macrame 7

Macrame Essentials 12

Types of macrame twine...............................13

Yarn for Macrame? 13

How to Knot in Macrame?..............................17

Material for macrame.................................19

Macrame material made of wood 21

Metal macrame material 21

Tools and aids for making macrame 22

Macrame in a few steps...............................23

Macrame knot techniques..............................25

Macrame Jewellery................................29

Make macrame jewelry yourself........................30

Material for a macrame jewellery 31

Decorating Macrame Jewellery 33

Macrame Projects 36

Shell Decoration.....................................36

Summer Shoes Decor 41

Hairclips with Shells................................44

Napkin Rings and Cloth...............................46

Macrame wall hanging.................................54

Macrame chain 60

Make Easter eggs with macrame 67

Flower Pots 72

Macrame keychain knot 78

Christmas pendants 90

Warming hair band 94

Lantern with macrame...100

Macrame Wallet 106

Macrame glasses case 112

Wall hanging lantern..118

Conclusion...124

Introduction to Macrame

Macrame is a knotting technique that originally came from the Orient. In fact, it was once the Crusaders and Moors who brought macrame to Europe as a technique. Back then, the works and macrame artworks were usually a little coarser than they are today. In the 80s and 90s macrame was hard to find anywhere apart from handicraft markets and traditional craftsmen in Spain or South America. For some time now, however, DIY macrame has been completely up to date again - after all, the braided works of art fit perfectly into the hip boho and vintage trend.

Macramé is a technical art of knots that allows you to beautifully decorate your interior with just bits of string and a little creativity. But that's not all! Necklace, cushion, bracelet, sculpture, everything is at hand.

A macrame is a work made from a series of knots. Said like that, it does not make you want but it is an art of the thread that allows very beautiful works. This ancestral technique begins with the Arab weavers. It dates from the 13th century and is based on making fabric with knots,

flat or in relief. This decorative art then spread widely in Europe.

@BENNILOVESMACRAME

Today, macrame evolves with the times and is modernized with the manufacture of small objects such as jewelry or decorative accessories thanks to the diversification of basic materials (scoubidou thread for example), you will see!

Macramé is still a huge trend. Before you start knotting, offcourse, you need the right macramé material. One thing in advance: One of the best things about macramé is that you basically only need very little material and that you can get it at very different locations such as hardware stores or craft shops. Today I'll show you what my previous macramé material favorites have been. Come along!

You've seen it everywhere for some time, macrame wall weaving is trendy. For a long time when we thought of macrame, we immediately had the image of our grandmothers and their macrame shawls that we found so old-fashioned. Yet macrame is really cool!

Macrame has evolved a lot, has modernized and has become today a real creative hobby with the manufacture of small objects such as necklaces, earrings or macrame bracelets , handbags, placemats or more decorative accessories.

Are you a beginner? It is best to start by weaving flat knots, simple and solid, which will allow you to make jewelry.

For the more experienced, you can opt for weaving knots in relief , which will give volume to your creations such as macrame suspensions, planters , cushion covers or even decorative sculptures.

Whatever object you want to achieve, thanks to the technique of macrame knots , you will have a multitude of possibilities.

By mastering the technique of macrame knots you will be able to make superb projects, and not only wall suspensions but also suspensions for flower pots, handbags and even tank top straps.

Macrame has been one of the top trends in DIY and hobby for some time now. No wonder: with the macrame technique, all kinds of objects can be knotted, from wall hangings to macrame jewelry to pillow cases - ideal for those who do not like working with filigree materials but want to see results as quickly as possible. But what exactly is macrame? Which macrame thread can I use best? And where can I find suitable macrame instructions for my own ideas? This book will clarify these and many other questions about macrame. There are also numerous tips and tricks further described for anyone who wants to learn macrame.

Would you like to make a macrame hanging basket, a macrame pendant or a macrame rug yourself? Then you can learn macrame quickly with our help. All you need for this are the most important types of knots: basic knots, square knots, rib knots, weaver knots and wave knots. Sounds complicated? All types of knots are explained in detail in the macrame instructions in our macrame books.

Before you start, however, you should cut the macrame string properly. This proves to be a little complicated with macrame for beginners. That is why you will always find precise information about how long the individual cords of the macrame yarn should be in good macrame instructions or in a professional macrame book. The exact macrame technique also plays a role: the tighter you knot and the thinner your macrame thread, the longer the cord should be. At least four times as long as the finished knot - this is the value that is usually recommended by experienced macrame professionals. Still not sure whether to tie tightly or loosely? Then it is best not to take any chances and cut the macrame tape so that it is ultimately five times as long,

Tip: Did you measure the macrame cord too short? No problem: you can glue on a suitable piece with a little transparent glue - just let it dry and then go on knotting as if nothing had happened.

I also recommend that you set up the workstation where you want to create individual works of art according to macrame instructions so that you can take a comfortable position when knotting and change it more often if necessary. This will prevent you from getting a stiff neck or back pain, for example. This may be less important for small jobs such as a macrame hanging basket or a macrame key ring, but the correct working position is even more important for large projects such as a macrame wall hanging, which you will probably work on for many hours.

Macrame Essentials

To make macrame projects, you will first need a base, called a knot holder, which can be a wooden stick, a piece of fabric or rope.

When using a wire or rope, it is often referred to as a carrier strand. There are a lot of online shops that offer it and they have selection of cotton macramé yarns that you will choose according to the work to be made. They also offer macrame threads in different colors and in several sizes ranging from 1.5mm to 6mm in diameter.

To facilitate the realization of your macrame creations, you can equip yourself with a pair of scissors, a macrame plate, preferably squared to help you in the knotting of the threads, pins with heads to fix the macrame thread and a tape measure.

The wooden rings will allow you to customize your works and create, for example, a dream catcher, a bracelet or decorations in round shapes to hang.

The wooden sticks , present on our online haberdashery, allow you to hang your works on the wall.

Types of macrame twine

- The classic macrame cord is made of cotton and is available in two versions, namely braided or twisted

- Twisted yarn is in turn available in twisted versions or in versions with single threads.

Advantages and disadvantages

I mostly work with twisted yarn, as this can fray the ends (to finish off the project) and it is often cheaper. In my opinion, braided yarn brings more calm to a macrame knotting and is, above all, easier to handle, so it is particularly suitable for beginners. If you still prefer to use twisted yarn, then go for a twisted version to start with.

Yarn for Macrame?

If you get creative and want to make a wall hanging, a table runner or a belt from macrame yourself, the most important material you need is off course the right macrame thread. Different types are possible:

- cotton thread

- jute tape

- hemp rope

- coconut

- thread - acrylic or nylon thread

Each of these yarns has various advantages and disadvantages for macrame: Natural materials are always welcome because they have a pleasant feel, have a good ecological balance and are usually even allergy-friendly. For example, cotton yarn is not only strong and tear-resistant, but also impresses with its soft surface structure. On the other hand, macrame yarn made of 100% cotton is also comparatively heavy - if you want to make particularly large macrame objects, this may need to be taken into account.

Info: It is recommended that everything that has to do with fashion and textile accessories is always made from macrame yarn made of cotton, because this material is easy to wash. For example, if you want to make a macrame vest, a macrame scarf or a macrame table runner yourself, you should use cotton thread to ensure that you can easily clean the macrame objects in the washing machine.

Jute ribbon, hemp rope and cord made of coconut fibers or sisal tend to have a rough structure, but convey a particularly natural character. Macrame objects made from these yarns are ideal to match the Boho and Nature styles. If, on the other hand, you want to make macrame for outside, you should concentrate on synthetic yarns. These can even withstand moisture without any problems and therefore look great not just for one summer. Anyone who opts for acrylic, nylon or polyester yarn for macramé can also opt for colored yarns. This makes for an atmospheric eye-catcher on an atmospherically illuminated terrace between lush flowers and lots of wood.

Macramé yarn comes in all possible strengths. My thinnest yarn is 1.5mm thick and my strongest 6mm. The thicker the yarn, the coarser the project naturally looks, but the faster you can knot larger areas. For a wall hanging I would always use at least 3 mm thick thread. The 1.5 mm thick thread is well suited for jewelry and other smaller projects. At the beginning you have to play a little with the yarn sizes in order to find the right size for your taste.

Colored yarn:

The yarn is also made from 100% recycled material and the choice of colors is really great. Several brands have beautiful yarn with colored wefts or gold threads on offer.

- 1.5 mm twisted thread in different colors
- 3 mm twisted yarn in different colors
- 3 mm braided yarn in different colors

Twisted standard thread:

- for "coarser" macrame projects cotton cord 5 mm (the thickness is more like 6 mm, very nice light natural white)

- the "Mittelding" cotton cord 3 mm   (also very nice light natural white)

- for finer macrame projects cotton thread 2 mm (solid natural white)

Other types of yarn suitable for macrame:

There are off course other, less classic types of yarn that can be used for macrame. People mostly like to use elastic jersey tape   for my macrame jewelry. Waxed cotton, leather or embroidery thread are often used for fine macrame bracelets. Synthetic fibers can also be useful, especially for projects that have their place outdoors or that should be very robust.

Tip: If you want to buy macrame yarn, you should not only pay attention to the material, but also to the strength: the thicker the macrame yarn, the better it is suitable for large objects with a few knots. Filigree work instead requires a rather thin thread with a thickness of less than 5 mm. Also, make sure to always order enough macrame yarn so that you don't have to order more while you are doing handicrafts.

How to Knot in Macrame?

If you look at macrame instructions in a macrame book, you will notice that in addition to the various aids and the required thread, many other utensils are used. Macrame rings, balls, beads or sticks are not only decorative accessories, but are also required as stabilizing elements for some macrame ideas:

- You need macrame rings if you have a macrame key ring or a macrame dream catcher want to tinker. Such a ring can also be used as a stabilizing and shaping aid for a macrame hanging basket or a round macrame wall hanging. There are macrame rings made of different materials. The following applies: the heavier the macrame object, the more stable the ring should be.

@BENNILOVESMACRAME

- Macrame beads and balls, on the other hand, are more of a decorative accessory with which you can spruce up your macrame work of art. With us you order wooden beads in bright colors or in a classic natural look. Glass beads or semi-precious stones and fresh water pearls can also be knotted into the macrame - this is how you individualize your macrame ideas and create works of art according to your taste.

- Macrame sticks are primarily important when you want to make a macrame wall hanging. After all, such a rod has to be used as a basic structure to tie the macrame cords to it. There are various options: For example, you can simply look for a suitable branch in a nearby forest or get a sturdy stick at the hardware store. Be careful not to choose the stick too thin or too thick. Extra tip: How about a colored stick for a cream-colored macrame? Simply paint and you will put a cheerful splash of color on your wall. Alternatively, you can stick washi tape and masking tape on the stick for the macrame - this way you can easily apply original patterns to the stick.

Material for macrame

When it comes to materials, macrame actually needs very few resources. Everything you need to get started right away can be conveniently ordered in our shop - from the right macrame thread to macrame rings, beads, balls and more. Many elements are optional and not for every macrame knot artwork need all the materials. Nevertheless, as with all handicrafts and handicrafts, it makes sense to equip yourself with all the necessary utensils from the outset so that you can implement the planned macrame ideas without interruption. Before going into more detail about which macrame yarn you should buy and which materials you can use for knotting, there is first a list of the most important tools and accessories that you should or should order from us in our shop for making macrame.

- tape measure
- scissors
- clothes rail
- needle
- hair comb
- hot glue gun
- glue

While the tape measure and scissors are needed to cut the macrame cord into suitable pieces, the clothes rail is helpful for securing the macrame artwork to it while you work on it. With a hair comb, finishing fringes can be combed smooth, whereas hot glue guns and hot glue as well as glue are ideal for gluing knots or threads. A crochet or knitting needle, on the other hand, can be used for tricky knotting and for fraying the macrame yarn.

Macrame material made of wood

In addition to the macrame thread, I can now call an impressive collection of wooden balls in various sizes and shapes my own. You can also get these from Amazon or any other online store.

Also wooden rings and rods (round or square) cannot be missing. These serve as a suspension. And nature also gives a lot on this topic. If you are disgusted with bugs, you can also heat the branches in the oven. Then you are on the safe side.

Metal macrame material

You need these accessories especially if you want to make beautiful macrame key rings yourself.

- gold-colored carabiner

- gold-colored key rings with hinged opening

- gold-colored normal key rings

- silver-colored carabiner

Tools and aids for making macrame

Off course, it is very important to have good scissors to cut the thread to the right length. A measuring tape or ruler will help you find this out. And in order not to forget the lengths, always write it in a notebook. Because finding the right lengths, in particular, was very difficult in the beginning, or it is still difficult with new projects because you need a lot of yarn (mostly more than expected!). To safely complete a macrame project or to secure knots, I often use textile glue or jewelry glue for macrame jewelry.

A hook or a clothes rail is suitable for hanging, if you would like to work while standing. However, I am sometimes very lazy and then tie the macrame to a chair or clamp the rod of the macrame in a chair and then work while sitting. The standing version is probably more back-friendly. I also find a macrame board   very practical for smaller projects and clipboards are very helpful for macrame bracelets.

Macrame in a few steps

- ### Making A Lark Knot On A Wooden Stick

To make a macrame wall decoration, first make a lark's knot. To do this, fold your 3 mm wire in 2 in the middle to form a loop. Pass both ends of the thread through the loop, wedging the stick in the middle.

- ### Making A Flat Knot

Then make an overhand knot with 4 lengths of thread, and therefore 2 lark's head knots. Start by taking the left strand and pass it above the 2 central strands and below the right strand. Then take the right strand and pass it below the center strands and through the loop of the left strand. Then tighten the two strands to form the overhand knot. Repeat the action in the other direction.

- ### Flat Knot - Variant 1

The reef knot may vary in effect depending on the number of supporting strands. With a 1.5 mm thread, make an overhand knot with 2 strands on several central strands over a substantial length.

- ### Flat Knot - Variant 2

The reef knot can also vary in effect depending on the number of actor strands. With a 1.5 mm thread, make a reef knot with 2 actor strands on each side. Then tie it on 2 central strands.

- **Flat Knot - Variant 3**

The reef knot can also vary in effect by alternating them on your load bearing strands. With a 3 mm thread, make an overhand knot with 2 actor strands on each side. Then tie it on 2 central strands for a substantial length.

- **Twisted Knot - Variant 4 Of The Reef Knot**

To obtain a twisted knot, create a half reef knot and always tie it in the same direction, making sure to have a fairly consistent length.

- **Making A Half Hitch Knot**

The half hitch knot is also ideal for creating suspensions. Produced in series, you will get a blanket stitch. It twists around the supporting strands. Make a chain of half hitches with the 6 mm thread. Form like a 4 with the actor strand around the supporting strand (s). Make sure to have a fairly substantial length for a better rendering.

- **Half-Key Knot - Variant**

Tie a large lark's knot on a ring support with 6 lengths to obtain 12 lengths. Tie half-hitch knots with 2 strands on 2 supporting strands. Then take two more strands in a row and tie 2 half-hitch knots again on the same supporting strands, until you make the entire length.

Macrame knot techniques

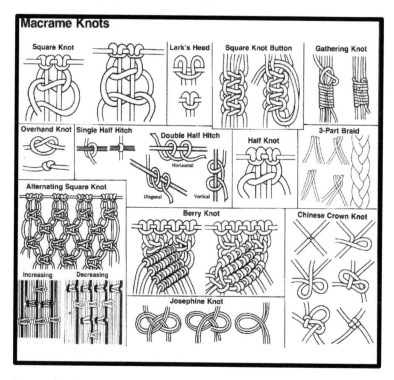

You will find a series of knots and their realization in this image to better understand how to tie them. There are a multitude of other knots but these are the basic knots to know.

1. The lark's knot

It is the knot that serves as the start of any macrame. You will use it to hang the strands of wire on your mounting bracket, whether it is a wooden stick, a driftwood branch or a circle with a shade.

Once this knot is made, you have two strands of thread ready for use. You can also tie the lark knot with a single thread.

2. Half hitch / blanket stitch

The half hitch is a very simple knot with which you can create slightly more elaborate combinations. The blanket stitch is quite simply a series of half hitches. The half hitch knot is the base for forming the chopsticks.

To form a half hitch, you will need a loose thread that is not hooked to the support. To form a half hitch, make a loop around the free thread. To form a blanket stitch, form several half hitches.

3. The horizontal / oblique / vertical strip

Chopsticks are formed from two half hitches, repeated on each strand of thread of the work.

Use a loose strand placed horizontally to form a horizontal wand.

For an oblique stick, make sure that your free thread is placed obliquely with your work and the half hitches should go down a little lower on each strand of thread. To form a vertical baguette, you use the loose yarn to make two half hitches on each strand of yarn in the work.

4. The flat knot / the alternating flat knot

The reef knot is always made with 4 strands of thread. This is another basic macrame knot to know how to make because once you master it, you can make very aesthetic variations of it like for example a series of alternating flat knots.

To create a square knot, you will create two half knots in two steps.

Step 1:

- The right thread goes over the two middle threads and then under the right thread
- The left thread goes under the two middle threads and then over the left thread

Step 2:

- The right thread goes under the two middle threads and over the right thread

- The left thread goes over the two middle threads and under the left thread

To alternate the flat knots, you just need to make a row of flat knots then leave two strands of thread free before starting the next row.

5. The half flat twisted knot

You just need to start tying an overhand knot, but instead of alternating the two steps, you will repeat step 1 or step 2. This series of half-knots will form a spiral.

It may happen that your thread is too short to finish your project. This is why you should always provide as much thread as the macrame tutorials recommend. If your wire is too short, don't be frustrated and hook an extension wire to it. You can hide this extension node with a wooden bead for example.

Macrame Jewellery

Macrame jewelry is all the rage: whether boho, vintage or hippie style - if you are out and about with a self-made macrame bracelet, a colorful anklet or a striking brooch, you will not only attract attention in summer. Macrame jewelry stands for lightness, naturalness and an unadulterated charm and is therefore particularly popular with young girls and women who are young at heart. But not only the women of creation find macrame jewelry attractive - more and more men are also wearing the self-made macrame bracelets or anklets as an expression of their individual fashion taste. Would you also like to tie your first macrame bracelet or are you already a macrame professional and looking for new inspiration and ideas for macrame jewellery? Then you are guaranteed to find something with us. In our shop you will not only discover everything to do with macrame, but also get numerous tips and tricks at hand.

Make macrame jewelry yourself

Macrame is a very old knotting technique that was developed in the Orient many centuries ago and has become known around the world over the years. Today macrame accessories and macrame jewelry are also made in China, Peru or in Northern Europe. The special thing about it: Anyone who has the right technology for macrame jewelry can create new works of art over and over again. And by using additional materials, you can create an infinite number of individual variations. For example, you can make macrame bracelets for different occasions - from festive and elegant to original and playful for the festival summer. But it is not just the simple technology and versatility that make macrame jewelry so popular: the natural look exuded by macrame bracelets and co. makes the homemade jewelry even popular with people who normally have little interest in jewellery.

Material for a macrame jewellery

If you want to make a macrame bracelet or a macrame anklet yourself, you need different materials. The most important thing is undoubtedly the macrame thread, which is the basis for making the macrame bracelet. Depending on how your individual piece of jewellery should look like, other materials and some accessories are required. The following equipments are recommended:

- Safety pin
- scissors
- Tape measure
- Glue
- Clasp

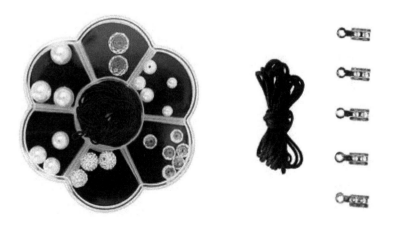

The needle can be used to make the macrame bracelet to fasten during weaving. This works best, for example, on a pillow that you have on your lap. Use scissors to cut the macrame thread; a tape measure will help determine the correct length beforehand. Glue, on the other hand, can be useful to seal the knots at the beginning and at the end of the macrame bracelet. Make sure, however, that the glue is transparent and quick-drying. You should also use it as sparingly as possible so that the look of the macrame jewelry is not impaired. You can attach a clasp to the macrame bracelet to be able to use a secure locking technology. Alternatively, you can do without this and simply attach the bracelet with a knot technique.

Yarn for macrame bracelets: which yarn is suitable for macrame jewelry?

Classic macrame yarns made of jute, sisal or hemp are less suitable for the production of fine macrame jewellery. The reason: The untreated natural fibers have a rough structure that many find to be too scratchy. In addition, macrame yarns made from these materials are too thick to make a filigree macrame bracelet. Instead, thinner cotton threads or embroidery floss is recommended. This can be divided into several threads so that you can, for example, make friendship bracelets in macrame style. Would you like to make it even easier for yourself? In our shop you can find suitable yarn for macrame jewellery to order.

Decorating Macrame Jewellery

Individual macrame jewelry is particularly noticeable because it can be embellished with countless materials. If you tie a bracelet in the macrame style, it can be worthwhile to incorporate various extras from the outset. Wooden beads, glass beads or plastic beads are just as suitable as rocailles beads or semi-precious stones and freshwater pearls. Pendants, sequins, feathers and bells can also be used in a macrame bracelet or in macrame jewellery to be woven. Whatever you like is allowed.

Tip: Do you love authentic pieces of jewelry and that is precisely why you are so interested in macrame jewellery? How about very personal charms and pendants that you associate with unforgettable memories? A shell from your last beach vacation, a pendant with a letter or a stone set in it - the list of possibilities is endless.

Making a macrame bracelet: How can you make a macrame bracelet yourself?

No matter whether you want to make a macrame bracelet, macrame hair accessories, a macrame brooch or other macrame jewelry yourself - you need appropriate instructions. Simply knotting different threads together in an unplanned way rarely leads to a nice result. You can order various macrame books from us, which also contain various tips about making macrame jewellery stand. It is important that you always tie the knots tightly or loosely. In the case of particularly filigree macrame bracelets, it is advisable to tie them firmly. This makes the bracelet even more robust and durable. In principle, a simple knot technique is enough to make versatile macrame bracelets. Here is a little guide:

Step 1: Knot four ribbons, each approx. One meter long, at the top

Step 2: Put the right band in a loop to the left over the two middle bands and pass it under the band on the left outside

Step 3: Pull the left band behind the two middle bands and then pull it forward through the loop formed by the right band

Step 4: Carefully pull the ends of the right and left straps tight so that a knot forms.

Tip: This simple way of tying a macrame bracelet can already be varied in two different techniques: Form the loop from the second step always with the ribbon on the far right, you get a macrame bracelet that is three-dimensionally curved like a spiral. If you switch the left and right side, you get a smooth and even macrame bracelet.

Macrame Projects

Shell Decoration

Summer is THE time for shell handicrafts and this year people are particularly keen to finally do something with the pieces of jewelry. If you don't have such a supply, you can off course also buy mussels. Here you have the advantage that these are usually already equipped with holes as a suspension. In any case, today I have 5 ideas for you, all of which are quite easy to implement, they only differ in the amount of time they take. Let's bring the summer home together and get started right away!

As a summer gem for the apartment, I made a wall hanging with various ribbons and shells. In order not to make the whole thing look too maritime, I "gilded" the shells. For this you need:

- gold foil
- application milk
- a brush for application.

How do you get holes in the shells?

For very thin clams, you can use a thick needle to carefully prick a hole through the shell. But that really only works with very few models. Otherwise I can give you a thin drill bit for

z. B. recommend the Dremel. With everything, you should be careful, as mussels can be very sharp when they break. Otherwise, as I said, there are also shells with holes to buy if that's too complicated for you.

Additional material for the shell wall hanging:

- Wooden stick (Here you can also use coniferous wood from the forest, from which the bark is removed.)
- Macrame yarn in different thicknesses (3 mm natural white   and 1.5 mm white with gold threads)
- Textile yarn z. B. from old T-shirts

This is how you make the shell wall hanging:

1. First I would come up with a rough concept for the wall hanging. For example, I proceeded in such a way that I started at a long point in the middle and got shorter and shorter with the "tinkling" to the left and right. But you can also stay on a line or make a diagonal across the length. This is off course entirely up to your imagination.

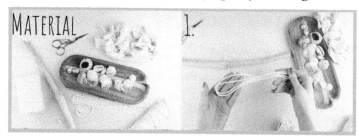

2. A series of simple square knots forms my center. You can find inspiration for the different types of knots and precise explanations in introduction above.

3. Then I complemented the whole thing symmetrically with more strings. I also like the addition of wide strips of fabric from an old T-shirt.

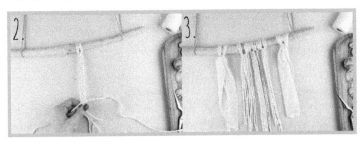

4. You can off course get really creative here. For example, I combed out some cords.

5. You can also add double-braided cords and wrapped k   n   o   t   s   .

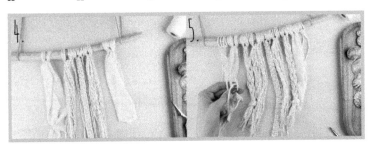

6. Finally, you can attach the (gold-plated) shells to your wall hanging with a thin thread.

And the pretty shell decoration in the boho look is ready. In our apartment she will probably find a nice place in the bathroom.

Summer Shoes Decor

Now we come to a nice DIY for your ultimate summer look. The main characters are a few simple white espadrilles that you can actually get in every store in the summer.

Other material for the summer shoes:

- Point drilled
- Shellfish with holes
- white thread and a needle

And this is how you pimp your summer shoes:

1. First you should place the point drill on the edge of the shoe. You can also pin this on the shoe to help. With my shoe model, it was possible to clamp the drill holes correctly under the edge, which gives a particularly h a r m o n i o u s   r e s u l t .

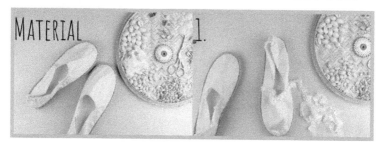

2. Now you can start sewing. I attached the thick part of the toe to the shoe with a simple lock stitch.
3. So the whole thing looks finished. Often the shoe consists of several layers of fabric. It works particularly well if you always sew in the middle layer. This gives the

whole thing a particularly professional look because you don't see any annoying seams inside.

4. You can then place the mussels in the gaps. You should fix these to the shoe with several loops of thread so that they don't come off so quickly.

5. Now you just have to repeat the whole thing with the 2nd fabric shoe and you have a couple of very individual s u m m e r   s h o e s .

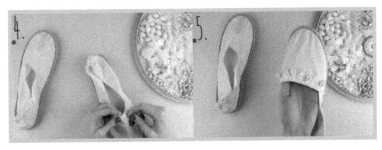

You can off course also use gold-colored shell pendants if you prefer it a bit more conspicuous, or a larger tip-drilled hole and maybe even beautiful summer colors.

Hairclips with Shells

Hair clips with seashells are really trendy right now. But you don't have to buy them, you can simply make them yourself and it doesn't even take 10 minutes.

What you need for the shell hair clip:

- a craft hair clip
- wider mussels (self-collected)
- gold-colored pearls
- hot glue
- Paper towel

And this is how you make the hair clip:

1. First you should arrange the mussels once on the clasp so that you know how much space you have available. With some kitchen paper clamped between the clasp, you can prevent the glue from running on the back. When the hot glue gun is preheated, you can get started. Tip: If you don't have a hot glue gun yet and want to stick something finer, there are also special models with finer tips. That will probably also be one of my next investments.

2. Then there are the pearls.

You are now done with your DIY clamshell clasp. If it doesn't look really chic, I don't know :-).

Last but not least, I have 2 more easy-peasy shell DIY ideas. A couple of gold-plated shells also make great earrings. To do this, simply attach the gold-plated shells to a pair of hoop earrings with an intermediate ring. You should then provide them with an additional layer of topcoat so that they are better protected against sweat etc. The other idea is a summery key ring. To do this, simply knot a row of square knots and a few more loose cords with thin macrame thread. The whole thing is rounded off with gold-colored shell pendants.

Napkin Rings and Cloth

For me, summer is the best time to dye Shibori and macrame is always possible anyway. So today I have a DIY project for you that perfectly combines the two: self-designed napkins with matching napkin rings. Another plus is that both the Shibori serviettes and the macrame serviette rings are really good beginner projects in their category and the material expenditure is also limited. Let's conjure up a summer table decoration together, let's go!

Material for napkin dyeing:

- Cloth napkins made of cotton
- Textile paint in shades of blue
- line
- other dyeing aids such as bowls, gloves
- scissors

Material for the napkin rings:

- 3 mm thick macrame thread z. B. in gray
- color matching sewing thread
- needle

Dye fabric napkins with a teardrop pattern

The cloth napkins should actually not be washed hotter than 30 ° C. However, I tested it on one beforehand and it only ran in very slightly. I would recommend that to you too, or use a textile dye for low temperatures. But now to the drop pattern, one of my favorite patterns:

1. First you cut a piece of yarn so that approx. 3 cm protrude left and right at the edge when you place the whole thing on the edge of the fabric.

2. Now you roll up the fabric more and more until a "sausage" is created.

3. Then make a simple overhang knot in the ends of the cord

4. and pull the whole thing together.

5. Then it's off to the dye bath.

6. Then you open the thread with the scissors

7. and can roll out the whole thing.

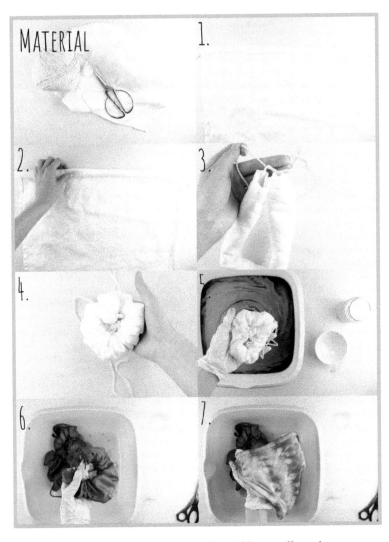

MATERIAL

1.

2.

3.

4.

5.

6.

7.

When you have washed the dyed napkins well again, you are done. I used 2 different shades of blue for my DIY cloth napkins. Now all that's missing is the matching napkin rings.

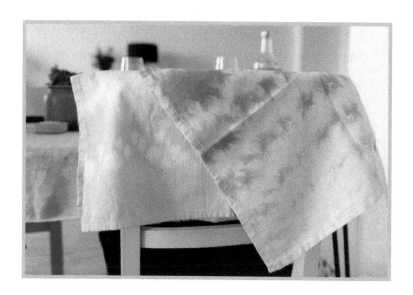

Make napkin rings with macrame

For the napkin rings we only need one macrame knot, namely the wave knot. If you want to find out more about knots. And this is how you make the napkin rings:

1. First you cut the yarn to size: You need a part of cord with a length of 50 cm and a part with a length of 200 cm. You then put the shorter cord in a loop and clamp it e.g. B. in a clipboard or attach it to a hook.

2. You attach the longer cord to the shorter one with a simple overhang knot. About the same amount of yarn should protrude on both sides.

3. The length of the loop should be 3 cm.

4. Now let's start with the wave knot. To do this, lead the right part of the cord **under** the central guide cords to the left and the left section of the cord **over** the guide cords to the right.

5. Then the whole thing is tightened well.

6. You continue to follow this rhythm. The rotation starts all by itself if you always tighten the cords well.

7. The correct length has been reached when the middle cords still protrude about 3 cm.

8. You now lead these cords through the loop and sew them up with a few stitches.

9. When you have closed the circle, you continue the wave knot so that the loop is knotted and you are back at the b   e   g   i   n   n   i   n   g   .

10. The protruding ends are now sewn and carefully

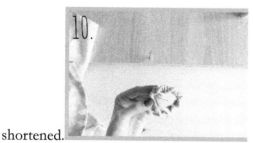

shortened.

And your great napkin ring is ready. With a little practice, the whole thing goes relatively quickly.

Make summer table decorations yourself

The fresh blue and the Shibori technique itself scream for me like summer. Off course, you can also color a matching table runner at the same time. The table decoration is perfect with a few beautiful flowers and lanterns. The possibilities here are really diverse and without a lot of material to implement.

Macrame wall hanging

I've done a lot of macrame projects in the meantime, but I didn't have a macrame wall hanging yet. Some time ago I felt like doing a classic macrame DIY and knotted a small, fine macrame wall hanging. You **only** have to **learn 3 knots** for this and the implementation is relatively quick. This makes the whole thing a **perfect beginner's project** so that you can put your first knotting skills to the test. Because a macrame wall hanging doesn't always have to be extremely complex to make a beautiful decorative piece.

Material:

- 3 mm thick macrame thread z. B. in the color Pearl   (20 cords with a length of approx. 1.60 m)
- Round wood stick from the hardware store
- Wooden beads

Aids:

- scissors
- Comb
- possibly saw to saw the suspension

Make macrame wall hanging yourself:

1. When you have cut the thread to the right length, you can attach the 1st cord to the log with the lark's head knot. If

you need more detailed instructions for the individual knots.

2. Repeat the whole thing with the remaining 19 strings. Tip: It is best to only saw your wooden stick to the desired length at the end of your knotting. So you can better assess the overall picture.

3. Now we start with the square knot. For this you lead the leftmost cord under the two middle cords to the right and the right cord over the middle cords to the left. Then tighten well!

4. Then you turn the whole thing around and lead the left cord over the two middle cords to the right and the right cord under the middle cords to the left.

5. Then tighten it again, which ends the first square knot.

6. This is how you knot the rest of the row with square knots to the end.

7. The 2nd row is offset below. The knotting scheme stays the same all the time.

8. For every further row you move one further inwards so that the whole thing tapers down at the end.

9. As an edge we now knot the diagonal rib knot. For this purpose, the leftmost cord is used as an inclined guide cord.

10. A loop with the adjacent cord is placed around this and tightened well.

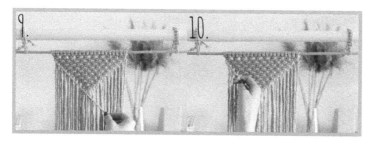

11. Then use the same adjacent string to form a loop again and tighten the whole thing again. So you keep knotting until you have reached the top and knot the right side analogously to the left side.

12. Then you put the square knot under the edge of the rib knot again, whereby I left out the 5th, 14th, 27th and 36th cord in order to thread a wooden bead. Tip: If you have trouble getting your thread through the bead hole, wrap some tape around it. This will hold the fringes together and allow the whole thing to be dented a little.

13. Underneath you knot another row of rib knots and continue the square knot-wooden ball combination.

14. Another row of rib knots follows as a conclusion.

15. Finally, you can cut the cords to length and then comb them out.

16. And your wall hanging is ready. If it bothers you that the fringes twist in, you can soak them in water for a while and then iron them carefully. Finally, you can attach a suspension with another string.

And your macrame wall hanging is ready:

Macrame chain

I want to put my time off with colorful macrame jewelry. It's made easy and a real highlight, a real statement chain. We only need one material and 3 basic macrame knots for this - doesn't that sound great? You can play really well with the technology and make earrings yourself in addition to necklaces. Let's get the good mood home while doing handicrafts, let's get started right away!

Material:

Jersey yarn (you can get this in a somewhat stiffer form , but you can also make this yourself from old T-shirts)

Aids:

- needle
- scissors

How to knot the macrame necklace:

1. The cord of your chain should be as long as your chain should ultimately be. If you want to use a macrame slide fastener like me, you should add another 10 cm. You also

need 8 more cords, each 80 cm long.

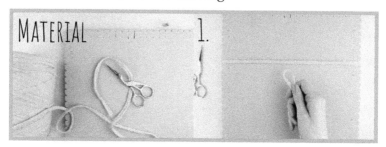

2. The 80 cm long cord is now doubled and attached to the support cord with the lark's head knot.

3. Repeat with the remaining 7 strings! (Attention: In the first pictures I attached one string too little.)

4. Now we start with the square knot: To do this, lead the left cord under the two middle cords to the right and the right cord over the middle cords to the left. Then tighten the whole thing well!

5. Then turn the whole thing over and run the left cord over the two middle cords to the right and the right cord under

the middle cords to the left. Tighten again well!

6. This is how you knot the rest of the row.

7. The 2nd row is knotted underneath offset.

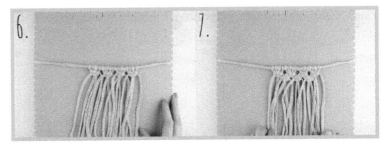

8. The 3rd row is knotted again like the 1st.

9. The 4th row follows the scheme of the 2nd row.

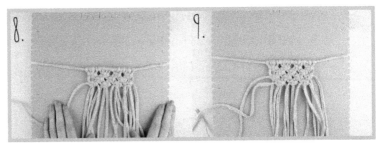

10. From the 5th row we let the whole thing come to a head. Now you only tie 2 knots in the middle

11. And finally a square knot as a point.

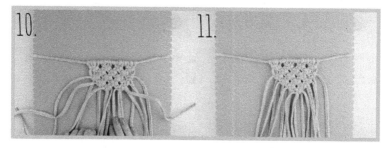

12. So that the chain is finished nicely, the rib knot now follows for one edge. For this, the leftmost cord is placed diagonally over the other cords and wrapped once with the adjacent cord

13. And then again with the same string.

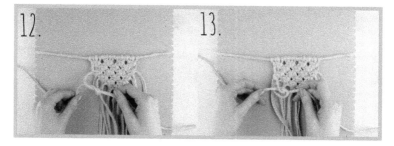

14. So you knot the row through to the tip.
15. The other side follows the same scheme.

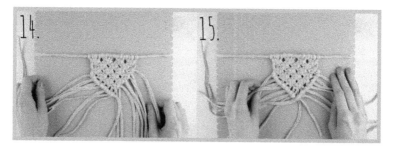

16. Both sides are connected with another rib knot.

17. Now you can shorten the ends of the cord as you like.

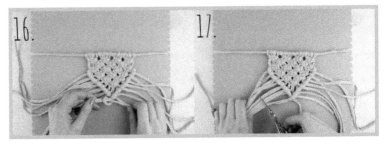

A macrame slide clasp is ideal for this chain. Then you don't have to be very careful with the length of the strap. I also think it's great that you can adapt the chain so wonderfully to the cutout shapes of the top. And if you want to give away the statement necklace, such a flexible clasp is off course extremely practical.

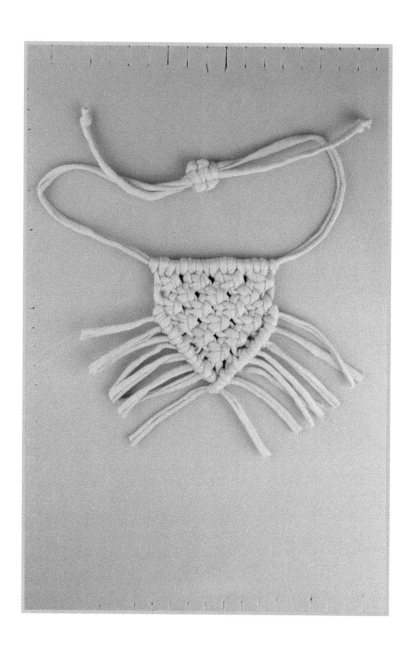

Make Easter eggs with macrame

With the crown knot we tie beautiful eggs to hang up. In connection with fruit branches or willows, this creates a completely natural Easter decoration. The crown knot is learned super quickly and you can use it for many beautiful DIY projects. Let's get started right away!

Material:

- 3 mm thick macrame thread in natural white
- colored embroidery thread
- Thread

Aids:

- needle
- scissors

And this is how you make the Easter eggs:

1. First the yarn is cut. You need 4 cords with a length of 120 cm each. These are brought together at the top with a simple knot. *Caution: Do not pull the knot too tight, it serves as an auxiliary knot and will be opened again later.*

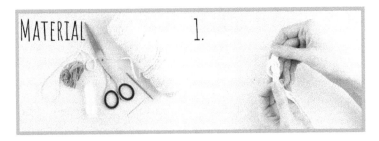

2. Now let's start with the crown knot. To do this, first lay all 4 cords in one direction.

3. The cord in the north is first placed with a loop over the cord in the east.

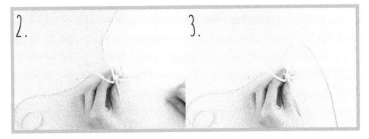

4. The cord in the east is then in turn laid over the cord in the south.

5. The cord in the south is then put back over the cord in the west, so that a "D" is created again.

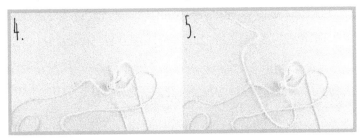

6. The last cord in the west is then led to the right.

7. You pull it through the "D" of the north cord.

8. Then you tighten the whole thing evenly and start over.

9. When you have reached the right length for your Easter eggs, you can stop knotting. The knot at the top should be untied now at the latest.

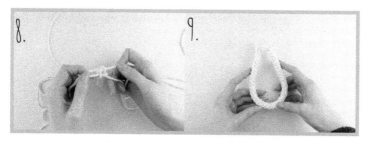

10. Now the ends are roughly sewn together with the thread and the protruding ends shortened.

11. Then you wrap the colored thread over the seams.

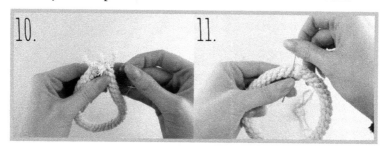

12. The end of the thread disappears into the winding.

13. When you have achieved a nice winding, the other end of the thread is shortened and also brought into the inside of the winding using a needle.

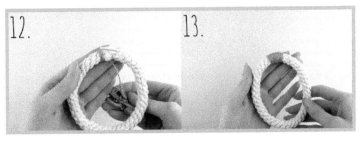

14. Finally, a thread is attached to the wrapping as a suspension. And your Easter egg is ready. The thick yarn gives it a certain stiffness and you can shape it well.

Flower Pots

This part shows how you can make small flower pots out of old glasses. B. can design for early bloomers. Off course, I use my favorite macrame technique, but I also have a simple DIY idea with wickerwork. Do you also feel like some fresh spring decoration? Then let's get started right away!

Material:
* Disposable glasses
* Jersey yarn

Aids:
* scissors
* towel

And this is how you design the flower pots:

1. First you attach a piece of jersey yarn to the top of the glass with a loop. Tip: If you want to keep all options open, take a long piece of the yarn and make a larger loop. So you can later attach the whole thing to glasses with a larger diameter.

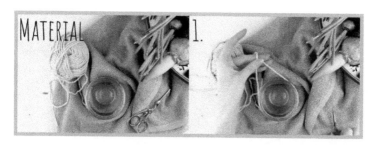

2. Now we use the lark's head knot to attach the shorter cords to the suspension. The thread has a length of approx. 30 cm. It is put in a loop and led from behind over the tether to the front. Tip: Place the glass on a crumpled cloth to protect it from rolling away.

3. The ends are then pulled through the loop and tightened.

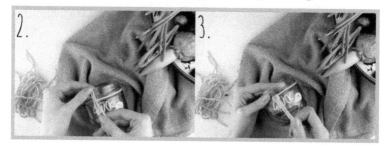

4. You repeat this with 11 more strings.

5. Now we start with the square knot. To do this, the left cord is passed to the right under the middle cords. The right cord is passed over the middle cords to the left.

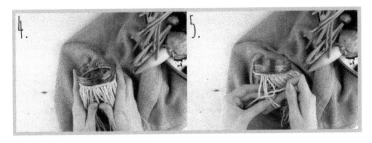

6. Then the left cord is passed over the middle cords to the right. The right cord is led to the left below the middle cords. Finally, tighten well.

7. You repeat this until you have a row of 6 square knots.

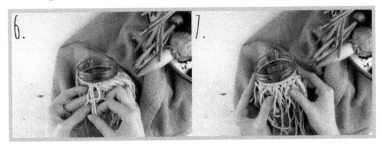

8. For the 2nd row, the square knot is offset under 2 square knots in the 1st row. The outermost 3 left cords are no longer used.

9. So you keep going until you get to the top.

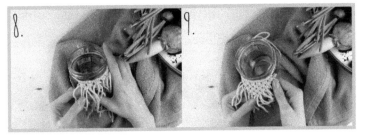

10. Now we use the rib knot to create a nice border. The left cord is used as a guide for this. The neighboring cord is wrapped around this from below.

11. A second loop is made with the same cord, which is then tightened well.

12. The next rib knot is made with the adjacent cord. You go on like this until you reach the top.

13. On the right side you also knot the edge and then you are d   o   n   e   !

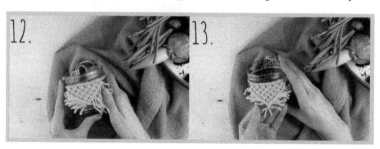

Off course, you decide for yourself whether you shorten the fringes.

Another variation is the one with the little flags, like a pennant chain for the flower pot. For this you use 8 cords and only knot 3 rows. The 1st row consists of 3 square knots. The next flag is tied directly to the first.

Macrame keychain knot

A macrame key ring is one of the more typical macrame projects. Why do I still find this so awesome? They are the perfect beginner DIYs in the macrame area, as you can perfectly try out the newly learned knots in any combination. In addition, you are done with the knot relatively quickly (A quick sense of achievement is always important) and you only need a little material. In this I'm going to show you 3 different versions of macrame key chains - let's get started right away!

Material:

- gold-colored carabiners
- 5 mm thick twisted macrame thread   (for heart charms)
- 3 mm thick braided macrame thread   (for the flag hanger)
- 2 mm thick twisted thread   (for pendants with pearls)
- Wooden beads

Tool:

- scissors
- Comb

1st version: key ring heart

The macrame keychain is really quick to make and the perfect little gift idea for the approaching Valentine's Day or other occasions when you want to express your affection.

Required nodes:

* Lark head knot
* Rib knot

That's how it works:

1. First you have to cut the twisted yarn. You need 4 cords with a length of 40 cm.

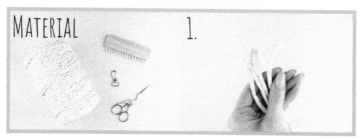

2. Then you put the cords twice in a loop and attach them to the carabiner with the lark's head knot.

3. Repeat with 3 more strings!

4. Now we use the rib knot in the diagonal variant. The left cord is used as the first passive cord for this. The cord next to it is wrapped around this from below over the cord.

5. Then tighten well!

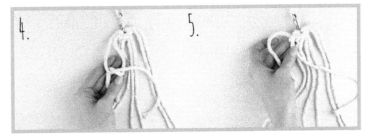

6. Then you wrap the same cord around the passive cord again. You repeat this with 2 more strings.

7. Then the string on the far right is used as a passive string.

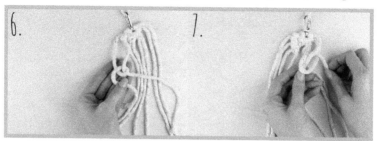

8. A total of 3 cords are also tied around these with the rib knot.

9. As a conclusion, the left and right sides are brought together with another winding knot.

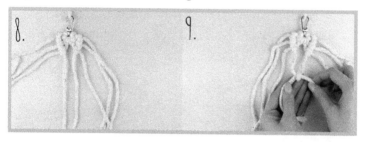

10. This creates a heart shape.

11. Finally, you can shorten the protruding cords and then comb them out. You can also wet the fringes and then comb them again to create a more even picture. This will release the twist of the cord.

2nd version: key ring flag

This macrame keyring is basically knotted in the same way as the first one. However, you knot more rows with this, so that a flat image in the shape of a flag results.

Required nodes:

- Lark head knot
- Rib knot

That's how it works:

1. Here, too, you need 4 cords with a length of 80 cm.

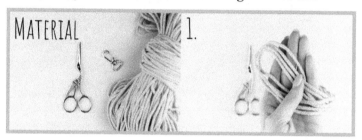

2. These are attached to the carabiner with the lark's head knot.

3. Now you wrap the second cord again around the cord on the far left.

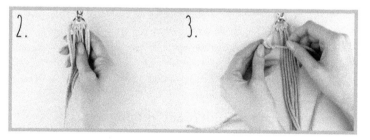

4. Tighten well and form a loop again with the same cord.

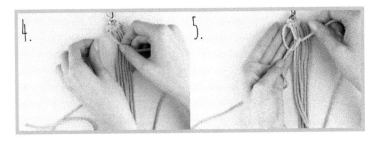

5. You repeat that with 2 more strings.

6. Now you make the next rib knot from the right side and knot diagonally downwards, until both sides meet again.

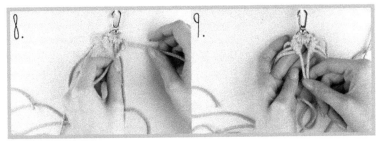

7. Another winding knot connects both sides.

8. The next row is then simply knotted under the first. For this purpose, the cord on the far left is used again as a

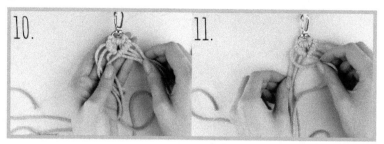

9. You knot to the middle and then knot the other side from the right. You go on like this until you have reached the desired length.

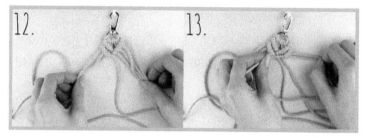

Your second key ring is ready, yay!

3rd version: macrame key-ring with pearl

Finally there is a macrame key ring with a square knot and pearl. You can also modify this wonderfully and add the already explained rib knot.

Required nodes:

- Lark head knot
- Square knot
- Rib knot
- Winding knot

That's how it works:

1. For this macrame keychain we use 4 cords of twisted yarn with a length of 80 cm.

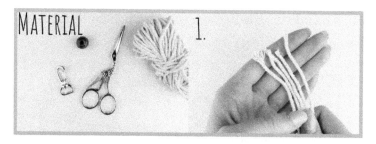

2. These are attached to the carabiner with the lark's head knot.

3. For the first square knot you take the first 4 ends of the cord. The left cord is passed under the passive cords in the middle to the right. The right cord is passed over the passive cords to the left.

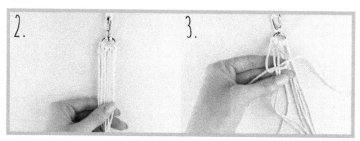

4. Pull the whole thing so tight that it connects to the lark's head knot.

5. Then do exactly the opposite and tighten the square knot

w   e   1   1   .

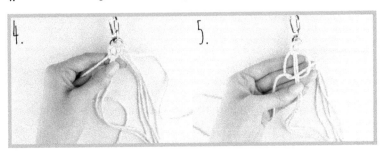

6. Repeat the whole thing with the other four strings.

7. The next square knot is knotted below it, offset. The 4 cords in the middle are used for this.

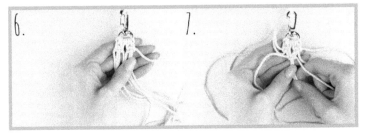

8. Then the pearl is pulled up and another middle square knot closes it.

9. Now, depending on your taste, you can knot further rows with square knots underneath.

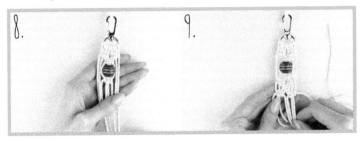

10. This macrame key-ring is finished with a winding knot. For this you need another 10 cm long piece of string. You then start with a 4 cm loop, which you place over the knotted ends and wrap the other end of the cord. The end of the loop protrudes slightly at the top.

11. After about 6 wraps, guide the loose end of the cord through the loop.

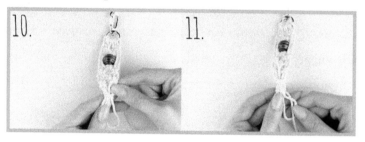

12. Finally, you can carefully pull the upper end so that the protruding lower end is "drawn in".

13. You are now done and can shorten and comb out the ends.

I think there is something for everyone with these 3 variants. As already mentioned: You can also modify the variants and combine the techniques. I especially like to give away the key rings with macrame knots, because they can be made quickly and a key ring can be used again and again. Such a key ring is particularly suitable as a small DIY housewarming gift. .

Christmas pendants

What are we missing for macrame luck this year? A macrame fir tree, off course! You can use this as a Christmas pendant for gifts and hang it up later on the Christmas tree or green - it fulfills a double function. The DIY fir trees are quickly knotted and also well suited for macrame beginners. You can practice the square knot (THE basic macrame knot!) In different variations on this macrame project. Another advantage: You only need 2 materials. Let's make great Christmas pendants right away!

Material:

- braided macramé yarn e.g. B. in dark green

- Wooden ring

Aids:

- scissors

And this is how you knot the Christmas pendant with macrame:

1. First you should fix the wooden ring to a solid object so that the cords are under tension and you can later tighten the knots. It starts again with a double stroke horizontally. I used 2 cords with a length of 1 m each for

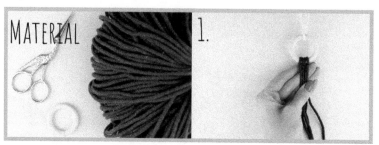

2. The two inner cords (passive cords) are the shorter. They should be a little longer than the Christmas tree should ultimately be long.

3. For the square knot you first lead the left cord over the passive cords to the right and the right cord under the passive cords to the left.

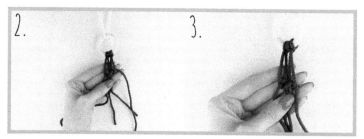

4. Tighten it well and then lead the left cord under the middle cords to the right and the right cord over the passive cords to the left.

5. Now put the next square knot at a distance of approx. 1.5 c m .

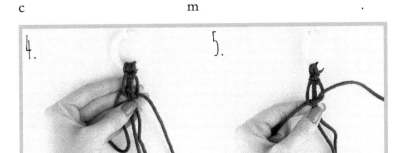

6. This time you do the exact opposite for the square knot.

7. Then you tighten the square knot again.

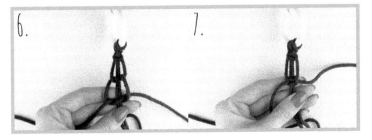

8. Then you push the square knot up (up to the 1st square knot). This is how the so-called picots, the little "ears", are created.

9. So you go on and increase the distance to the previous square knot step by step,

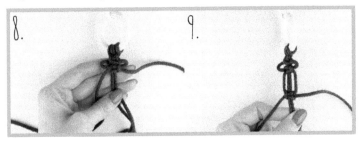

10. So that the branches of the fir tree enlarge towards the bottom.

11. When you have reached your desired size, you tie another square knot as a trunk by not forming picots, but simply leaving the square knot at the knot.

12. Finally, the protruding ends are shortened.

And your Christmas macrame pendants are ready

Warming hair band

The time has come: we have arrived in the dreary autumn weather. And you too may have reached for a hat or scarf. Reason enough for me to take action myself. I knotted a hair band with macrame, which not only looks very nice, but also has a warming effect. You only need a little material and two types of knots for your individual headband. Anyway, I'm a big fan of simply making accessories myself - you too? Then let's get started right away!

Material:

- Jersey yarn
    - in gray
    - in salmon
- matching color yarn

Aids:

- scissors
- needle

A macrame board is also very practical for this DIY, but not a must.

Knot hair band - this is how it works:

1. The hair band consists of a total of 10 strings, each 2.50 m long. Off course, you have to cut these to size first. Tip: Use a little more yarn for your 1st hair band. Since every head is different in size, I can of course not give you any exact information. I would describe my head size as narrow to normal. You can then clamp them twice in the macrame board. Or you glue them e.g. B. firmly on a table with tape.

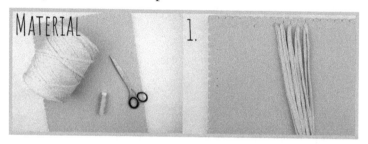

2. For this macrame DIY we again use the rib knot intensively and later also the square knot. We start with the rib knot: For this, the cord on the outside left is used as a passive cord and placed diagonally over the other cords. The cord next to it (or below it for macrame board users) is now wrapped around the passive cord

3. and then tightened. Then the whole thing is repeated again with the same string.

4. You do this with 3 more strings.

5. Now you start the whole thing again from the right. The passive cord is now the one on the far right.

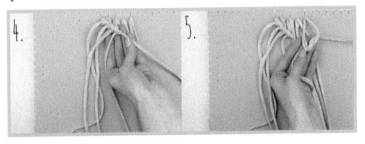

6. The cords lying next to it are knotted around these again. Make sure that you keep the angle as with the left part.

7. When you have knotted 4 cords, the whole thing meets in the middle.

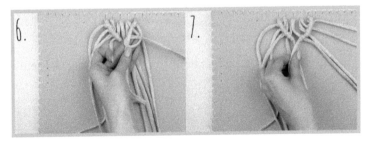

8. To create a transition, the right passive cord is now knotted to the active cord and around the left passive cord.

9. You now follow the line downwards by using the right cords again.

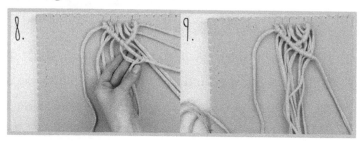

10. The knotting continues in the same way to the bottom left.

11. Now you knot the active cords in the middle to form a square knot. The 4 cords in the middle now serve as passive cords and are knotted with the 2 outer cords. The right cords are brought up over the passive cords and the left cords under the passive cords.

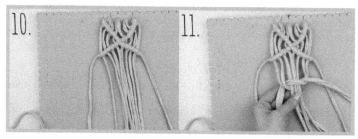

12. Then the whole thing is turned around.

13. When the square knot is well tightened, continue with the rib knot

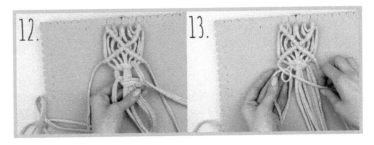

14. And so basically covers the square knot.

15. If both knots cross again, you use the passive cord on the right as a guide cord and form the knot with the cords on the left. It looks like the one string is always on top.

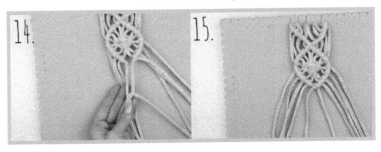

16. So you go ahead and end with a square knot. I created 7 "honeycombs". But of course it depends on how tightly you knot and how diagonally. *Tip: If the headband is for you, you should always put it on from time to time to see if you can get there with the cord.*

17. Now both ends are knotted together. For this you use the winding knot again to connect the sides. You also pull the cords from the other side through the square knot. Tip: If you need a little more length, you can cheat a little here and knot the last honeycomb a little more

generously. You won't see it later when it's down at the back of the head.

18. Finally, sew the whole thing together at the overlaps on the inside and then cut off the protruding ends.

And your self-made macrame headband is ready - if that's not great.

Lantern with macrame

This time I knotted different leaves and so a wonderful autumn lantern was created. Because warm candlelight is simply part of the autumn decoration for me. The DIY lanterns are beautifully simple and the candlelight shines really great through the macrame. Another plus point: You only need two materials and two types of knots for the autumn wind light. Let's knot right away and make beautiful autumn decorations together!

Material:

- larger glass (e.g. mason jar)

- Macrame thread, 3 mm thick

    o   in gray

    o   in pink

Aids:

- scissors

- possibly macrame board or tape

Make macrame lantern yourself:

1. First the yarn is cut to size. For the sheet you need 11 pieces with a length of 80 cm. 1 piece (= carrier cord) should be slightly larger in length than the circumference

of your glass (so that there is still some space for a knot).

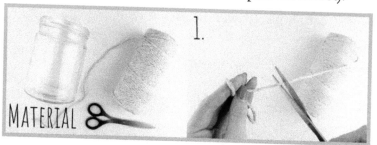

2. Then let's start knotting. You can also tie the macrame to the glass, which I found a little awkward. That's why I tightened the strap with some tape (a macrame board also works well here). As always, you start with the lark's head knot. If you want to familiarize yourself with the basic knots first, you can search a lot of material online

3. When you have attached the 11 cords to the carrier cord, the sixth cord is placed over the others to the right (= passive cord).

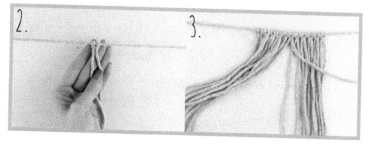

4. For this macrame project we are going to use the sloping rib knot. First you wrap the right cord from the passive cord around it from bottom to top.

5. The whole thing is tightened well and then the end of the cord is placed over the passive cord,

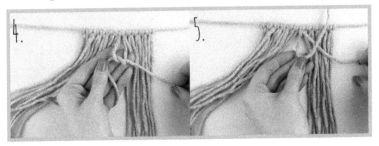

6. and led back down around it. Then tighten again well!

7. Now the procedure is repeated with the adjacent string.

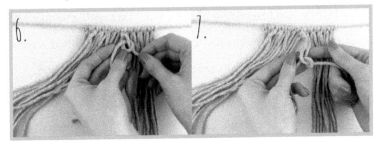

8. You should keep an eye on the incline of the guide line.

9. You continue like this until you have knotted a total of 8 strings. Then the direction is changed to the left and the guide cord is placed on the other cords accordingly.

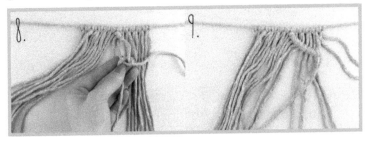

10. Now you follow the knotting scheme

11. with the difference that the whole thing is now left-wing.

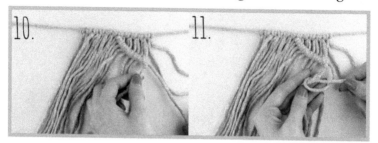

12. Tighten the knots again! At the end of this row you have knotted 5 strings diagonally downwards to the left.

13. Then the direction is changed back to the bottom right.

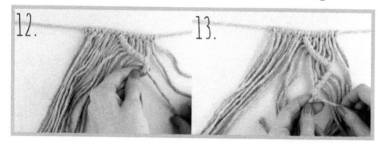

14. A total of 7 strings are now linked. 5 of these have already been used before, 2 more are added on the edge. The direction is now changed again to the bottom left

15. and so formed the conclusion of the sheet. For this you knot almost horizontally to the left. In this case, 10 cords

are tied with the rib knot.

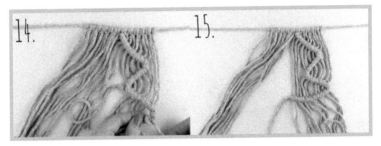

16. The whole thing is now repeated mirror-inverted with the other side of the sheet.

17. Finally, you bring both sides together with a few rib knots and you can knot a leaf style.

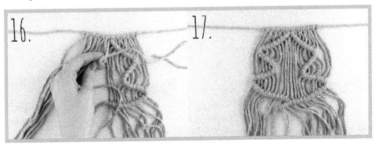

18. You can now fill up the sides with more strings as soon as you have knotted the strap around the glass. This way you can see better how many lines you need to fill out.

And your homemade lantern is ready! Making individual autumn decorations yourself can be so easy.

Macrame Wallet

Your fingers just always want to have something to do? I will show you how you can use the square knot to make a simple wallet yourself. For me, this DIY wallet is the typical "vacation wallet". Because on vacation you don't need 10 different cards and you usually don't have tons of cash with you, at least that's the case with me. That's why I colored the wallet with summery colors. If you are already in the autumn mood, you can of course also use other textile colors or leave the whole thing natural. We only need a small amount of material and the DIY is again ideal for macrame beginners. Let's get started right away!

Material:

- Macrame thread
- zipper
- Thread
- optional: tape and textile paint for spraying

Aids:

- scissors
- needle

Make your own wallet - this is how you proceed:

Note: You make the "wallet basic structure" just like the macrame glasses case with more cords, so I won't explain the procedure in great detail here. So if you want to have a more detailed description of the knotting, take a look there.

1. In the first step you have to cut the macrame thread. I used a cord with a length of 50 cm and 34 cords each 80 cm for my wallet.

2. First you fasten one of the longer cords horizontally to the shorter cord with half a twist.

3. You continue like this until you have lined up all 34 strings. (The following pictures are only examples.)

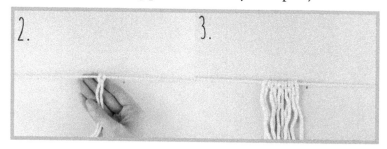

4. Now let's start with the knot. For the square knot you lead the right cord over the guide cords to the left and the left cord under the guide cords to the right. Then the whole thing is turned around.

5. The knot is then tightened well.

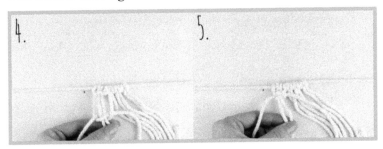

6. When you have finished the first row of square knots, the next row is tied underneath. With another square you close the whole thing. So you knot a total of 11 rows.

7. Then the underside is already made with a simple double knot. Make sure that you always tie the parallel cords so that there are no holes.

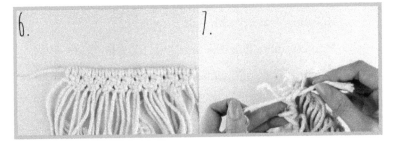

8. You can then shorten and fray the ends.

9. Then the zipper is sewn in with a few simple stitches.

And your DIY wallet is ready in the raw version.

Customize macrame wallets even more

If you like to design your wallet individually, I have a few more tips for you: I made another tassel and attached it to the side. If you don't like tassels, you can simply knot the protruding ends, fix them with some textile glue and shorten them. As a highlight, I designed my wallet with textile paint to spray on. For this I first masked one side with some tape and sprayed the lower area and the tassel. When the whole thing is dry, you can treat the upper side with the lighter fabric dye. There are of course no limits to your imagination.

Make a variety of macrame accessories with square knots

You already notice - you can make an incredible number of great and practical accessories with macrame and you actually only need the square knot. For example, following these instructions, you could also tie a larger cosmetic bag by simply using more and longer cords.

Macrame glasses case

I have new step-by-step instructions for you: a glasses case that you can knot with macrame, yeah. It's really practical and looks pretty too. This macrame DIY is also ideal as a beginner's project, as you basically only use the square knot to knot. I tied my glasses case while I was on vacation by the pool - maybe that's a good idea for you too?! You only need a small amount of material that is easy to transport. Let's make a great glasses case ourselves!

Material:

- Macrame thread (3 mm thick)

- optional colored embroidery thread for a tassel

- Textile glue

Aids:

- Scissors

Make your own glasses case with the square knot:

1. First you have to cut the macrame thread as usual. This time you need a piece of cord (approx. 60 cm long) and 24 pieces with a length of 1.60 m each. In the end, my glasses case became approx. 17 cm long. Tip: Just see how big your glasses are and adjust the measurements

accordingly and remember: better too much than
annoying later.

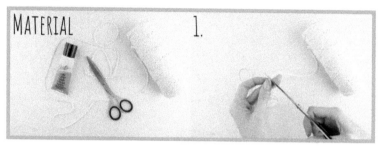

2. Now you stretch the 60 cm long cord z. B. with 2 clamps
   on a board so that it hangs tight. Then you attach the first
   string with half a twist horizontally to this tightly pulled
   string.

3. You repeat this with the remaining 23 strings.

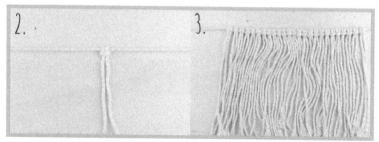

4. Now the square knot is used again. You connect 2 pairs
   of cords by leading the cord on the right over two guide
   cords to the left. The left cord is passed under the guide
   cords to the right.

5. Then you turn the whole thing around.

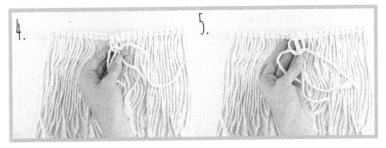

6. The knot is tightened nicely.

7. You repeat the square knot with the remaining strings. The second row is knotted below it offset. This time the square knots are also tied as close together as possible. Not like the macrame bag, for example, where we intentionally left an even gap.

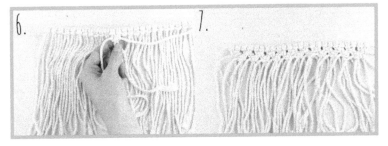

8. At the end of the second row, I would also start closing the glasses case by connecting the two leftover strings with a square knot.

9. The protruding ends of the cord, to which all other cords are attached, you simply let hang down; we will need this

later.

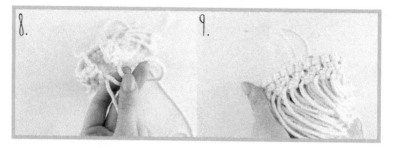

10. So you keep knotting until you have reached your desired length. I ended up tying 22 rows of square knots.

11. To close the glasses case, you knot the opposite ends of the cord with two overhang knots. *Tip: Take this step by step so that you don't forget any string.*

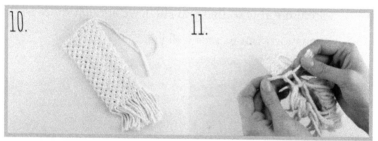

12. Finally, cut off the excess ends of the cord.

13. I then secured the knots again with some textile glue to really prevent them from opening. *Tip: As an alternative to steps 11-13, you can also connect the opposite sides with another*

square knot by taking the cords twice and then leaving the fringes.

14. When the glue has dried well, you can turn your DIY glasses case inside out and the lower edge disappears inwards.

15. Now we come to the closure. For this you pull the loose cords through the opposite hole between 2 square knots and knot this so that you still have enough space to transport your glasses well inside.

16. You can now cover this knot with a nice tassel.

And then the glasses case is knotted with macrame - great, isn't it? I admit it takes a while to make it, but the result definitely makes up for it, because only you have such an individual glasses case?

As an alternative to the tassel, you can also use the monkey fist knot to tighten the clasp.

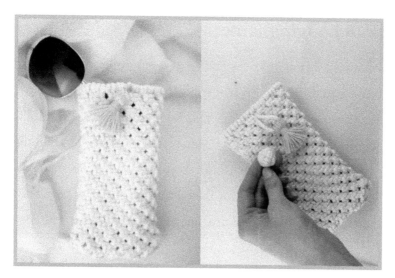

And another tip: If you want to protect your glasses even more, you can attach a felt insert to the inside of the glasses case.

Wall hanging lantern

I knotted different leaves and so a wonderful autumn lantern was created. Because warm candlelight is simply part of the autumn decoration for me. The DIY lanterns are beautifully simple and the candlelight shines really great through the macrame. Another plus point: You only need two materials and two types of knots for the autumn wind light. Let's knot right away and make beautiful autumn decorations together!

Material:

- larger glass (e.g. mason jar)
- Macrame thread, 3 mm thick
    - in gray
    - in pink

Aids:

- scissors
- possibly macrame board or tape

Make macrame lantern yourself:

1. First the yarn is cut to size. For the sheet you need 11 pieces with a length of 80 cm. 1 piece (= carrier cord) should be slightly larger in length than the circumference

of your glass (so that there is still some space for a knot).

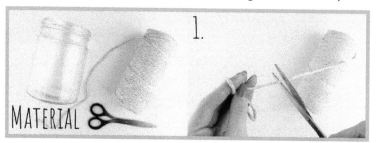

2. Then let's start knotting. You can also tie the macrame to the glass, which I found a little awkward. That's why I tightened the strap with some tape (a macrame board also works well here). As always, you start with the lark's head knot.

3. When you have attached the 11 cords to the carrier cord, the sixth cord is placed over the others to the right (= passive cord).

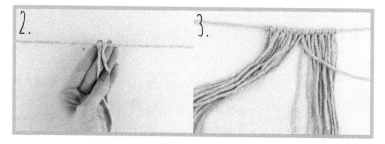

4. For this macrame project we are going to use the sloping rib knot. First you wrap the right cord from the passive cord around it from bottom to top.

5. The whole thing is tightened well and then the end of the cord is placed over the passive cord,

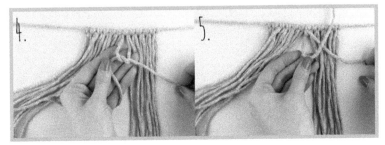

6. and led back down around it. Then tighten again well!
7. Now the procedure is repeated with the adjacent string.

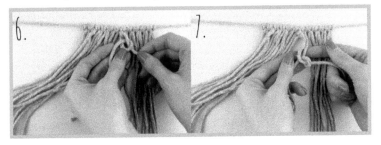

8. You should keep an eye on the incline of the guide line.
9. You continue like this until you have knotted a total of 8 strings. Then the direction is changed to the left and the guide cord is placed on the other cords accordingly.

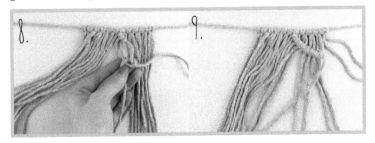

10. Now you follow the knotting scheme

11. with the difference that the whole thing is now left-wing.

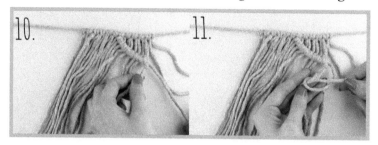

12. Tighten the knots again! At the end of this row you have knotted 5 strings diagonally downwards to the left.

13. Then the direction is changed back to the bottom right.

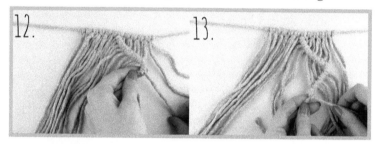

14. A total of 7 strings are now linked. 5 of these have already been used before, 2 more are added on the edge. The direction is now changed again to the bottom left

15. and so formed the conclusion of the sheet. For this you knot almost horizontally to the left. In this case, 10 cords

are tied with the rib knot.

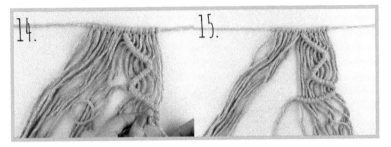

16. The whole thing is now repeated mirror-inverted with the other side of the sheet.

17. Finally, you bring both sides together with a few rib knots and you can knot a leaf style.

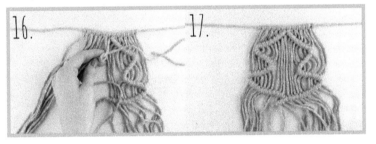

18. You can now fill up the sides with more strings as soon as you have knotted the strap around the glass. This way you can see better how many lines you need to fill out.

And your homemade lantern is ready! Making individual autumn decorations yourself can be so easy.

Conclusion

I know that there are a lot of talented craftsmen and craftswomen (Specially Macrame experts) out there, but how many of you are as good at selling your designs as you are at creating them?

To start and run a profitable craft business, you must — of course — have a specific product which can be made and sold. The important thing is that there should be a demand for the things that you can make at the prices for which you want them to sell. If you enjoy doing something for which you know there is little demand or if your product cannot be priced profitably, keep it as a hobby and start a business with some other item.

In case of Macrame selling startup business, I recommend to start selling your crafts online. There are numerous online platforms available including Shopify, eBay and many more. Also I suggest to start social media marketing at smaller level because SM marketing style is very powerful for this type of products. You can make an Instagram account of Facebook page to promote your Macrame crafts.

Lightning Source UK Ltd.
Milton Keynes UK
UKHW021020181120
373617UK00006B/74